Salmon Cookbook

Salmon Recipe Book with Yummy Collection of Salmon Recipes

Salmon Tastes Book 5

By Brendan Fawn

Salmon with Couscous and Parsley 53

Salmon with Sweet Potatoes and Pineapples 55

Salmon and Cuscus 57

Kippered Salmon with Dill 59

Spicy Kippered Salmon wit Parsley 61

Salmon in Foil with Amaranth and Avocado Sauce 62

Salmon in Orange Juice with Walnuts and Sesame Seeds 64

Salmon Cutlets with Quinoa 66

Salmon Cutlets with Cashews and Cuscus 68

Salmon with Broccoli, Peas and Noodles 70

Salmon, Tomatoes and Garlic Pasta with Romano Cheese 72

Baked Salmon with Sweet Potatoes, Herbs, Plums and Romano Cheese 74

Salmon Balls with Oregano and Lemon 75

Salmon Salad with Almonds and Oranges 77

Salmon Balls with Spanish Herbs and Walnuts 78

Salmon with Noodles, Tomatoes and Romano Cheese 80

Salmon with Spaghetti and Pears 82

Beans with Salmon, Pork and Cucumbers 83

Baked Salmon with Zucchini Spaghetti and Cottage Cheese 85

Salmon Balls with Onions 87

Marinated Salmon with Nutmeg 89

Introduction

This salmon cookbook was created for people who want to change eating routine and consume more healthy salmon.

This fish has a lot of advantages. Salmon is good for the health of the skin, nervous and digestive systems, regulates blood sugar and is an antioxidant. What is more, omega-3 fatty acids, which are found in large quantities in salmon, can affect person's biological aging.

This cookbook includes various salmon recipes mainly with vegetables, but also with meat, fish or nuts. In this salmon cookbook, you will find interesting and delicious salmon recipes that will inspire you to prepare tasty salmon dishes.

Often you should just use your imagination because actually there are no limits. And remember, this salmon cookbook hasn't all the recipes because it was created to inspire you to discover a colorful world of salmon cooking!

Moreover, you don't need to be a professional 28 Michelin Star chef to use salmon recipes from this cooking book and to prepare food for yourself, your friends or your family. I would like to encourage you to test new salmon recipes and to experiment adding your own flavors!

The Most Valuable Fish - Salmon

It is known that already in the Middle Ages, salmon was popular on European, Scottish and Australian shores. It was harvested in the summer, dried and smoked for the winter.

Salmon lives along the coasts of the North Atlantic and Pacific Ocean; it is bred in the Great Lakes of North America. As a rule, salmon is hatched in fresh water, migrates to the ocean, and then returns to fresh water to spawn.

The meat of this fish is considered a delicacy, but it is quite affordable. Salmon is a large fish with tender meat. The taste of salmon is very soft and delicate. The color of the meat can be from orange to bright red, depending on the habitat, nutrition and other factors.

From salmon you can cook a lot of tasty and healthy dishes - from simple to exotic. Salmon can be baked, fried, stewed or cooked. Original holiday dishes are prepared from salmon pre-pickled with herbs and spices. For example, salmon fillet can be baked with shrimps and vegetables in puff pastry.

"To preserve the natural taste of fish, it is best to cook, bake or stew it with vegetables and herbs. Salmon can be grilled and served with a variety of sauces".

Salmon goes well with sweet and sour, spicy and even sweet fruit sauces. Salmon meat is added to soups and broths. In addition, a huge number of salads can be prepared from salmon. For instance, a salad of tomatoes, cucumbers, garlic, eggs and canned salmon. In general, there are a lot of recipes for salads with canned salmon and you will find few of them in this cookbook. It can be combined with cheese, fresh vegetables, olives, eggs, and legumes.

Salmon meat can also be fried. The original will be salmon fried in mustard with herbs. Salmon can be baked in the oven in a foil with lemon juice and herbs. This fish goes well with potatoes, pasta and vegetables. Salmon meat is often salted. Lightly salted salmon is added to salads, rolls and sushi. Salmon could be served as a snack. Salted salmon goes well with butter; sandwiches are often prepared with it.

Salmon meat is rich in vitamin B1, PP, as well as potassium, phosphorus, chromium.

Phosphoric acid is involved in the construction of numerous enzymes (phosphatases) - the main engines of chemical reactions of cells.

The fabric of our skeleton consists of phosphate salts.

"Salmon is good for the health of the skin and mucous membranes, nervous and digestive systems, regulates blood sugar, is an antioxidant".

Omega-3 fatty acids, which are found in large quantities in salmon, can affect a person's biological aging. These substances prevent the shortening of the end sections of chromosomes, thereby slowing down aging. Fatty acids have a positive effect on brain cells, helping to prevent the development of memory and attention problems caused by age or illness. Experiments with mice have shown that a diet rich in omega-3 extends the life by one third.

Calories and nutritional value of salmon

Calories - 153 kcal.

Salmon nutritional value: proteins - 20 g, fats - 8.1 g, carbohydrates - 0 g

Kitchen Tools That You Will Need to Prepare Homemade Salmon Recipes

To prepare homemade salmon recipes you will need to have the right tools in your kitchen. The following list of kitchen utensils will help you.

Food scale

The food scale is the main tool. You will use it to measure any food and it will always show you the quantity of ingredients that you need.

Food processor or blender

Having a food processor or blender is important. It will help you to process, pulse, and blend various ingredients.

Electric hand mixer

Electric hand mixer will save your energy and of course time, especially when preparing salmon recipes where you often need to combine various ingredients and whisk the eggs.

Pot or saucepan

Having a large pot, saucepan or bowl in your kitchen is important for preparing salmon recipes because you will melt, mix, combine, keep and boil all the ingredients there.

Skillet or wok

Having a big skillet or wok in your kitchen is crucial because you will fry and stew your salmon, shrimps, vegetables and fruits alone, combined and with various ingredients such as wine or oil.

Knife sharpening stone or sharp knife

When preparing salmon dishes you often need to cut, slice or dice. In this case, having a sharp blade in your kitchen will save you a lot of time and frustrations because you will finish cutting up your salmon or vegetables much faster than you would if using a dull knife.

Baking pan

Baking pan is extremely important because you will bake your salmon and vegetables there.

The following chapters contain delicious salmon recipes that will have your taste buds come to life!

Salmon Recipes

Salmon Soup with Cabbage and Croutons

Prep Time: 20 min. | Cooking Time: 55 min. | Servings: 5

Ingredients:

25 oz salmon fillets
2 cups of cabbage, chopped
4 onions, peeled and chopped
1 baguette or white bread
2 cups of vegetable broth
4 cups of water
5 cloves of garlic, chopped
2 teaspoons herbs
5 tablespoons Olive oil
salt and pepper
1 bunch of parsley, chopped

How to Cook:

1. In a pot, heat the Olive oil and fry the chopped onions with the garlic for 5-10 minutes until clear and caramelized. Then mix in the salmon, salt and pepper. Pour the meat broth and boil it covered for about 25 minutes.
2. Cut the baguette or white bread into the small cubes and toss them with the salt, pepper and herbs. Preheat the oven to 250°-270° Fahrenheit and place the baguette cubes on a baking sheet. Bake the croutons for about 10-15 minutes until golden brown and crispy.
3. After 20 minutes add in the cabbage and all the remaining ingredients. Then reduce the heat and continue to boil for around 15 minutes but don't forget to skim the foam from the soup.
4. Spoon the croutons and sprinkle the chopped parsley on top. Portion the soup into four bowls or mugs and serve with the cream.

Nutritional Information:

Calories: 224; Total fat: 49 oz; Total carbohydrates: 58 oz; Protein: 36 oz

Veggies and Salmon Bouillon

Prep Time: 20 min. | Cooking Time: 40 min. | Servings: 4

Ingredients:

20 oz salmon, cubed
10 potatoes, peeled
2 onions, peeled
5 garlic cloves
10 oz unsalted butter
2 carrots, peeled
2 tablespoons soy sauce
2 tablespoons sunflower oil
salt and pepper
Herbs de Provence

How to Cook:

1. In a skillet or wok, melt the unsalted butter and fry the salmon for 20 minutes until half-cooked and crispy. Then pour some water to stew until light brown color.
2. Remember, don't chop or cut the vegetables, it is important in this type of bouillon. In a pot, heat the water and add in all the vegetables and the butter-salmon mixture. Then reduce the heat and continue to boil for around 30 minutes but don't forget to skim the foam from the bouillon.
3. Add in the salt and pepper. Portion the veggies and salmon bouillon into two bowls or mugs and dollop each bowl with the Herbs de Provence. Serve the

veggies and salmon bouillon with the wheat bread! Remember that this dish should be served warm.

Nutritional Information:

Calories: 265; Total fat: 47 oz; Total carbohydrates: 57 oz; Protein: 37 oz

Pumpkin-Salmon Soup with Croutons

Prep Time: 15 min. | Cooking Time: 65 min. | Servings: 3

Ingredients:

20 oz salmon, cubed
1 cup of pumpkin, peeled and diced
4 onions, peeled and chopped
1 baguette or white bread
2 cups of vegetable broth
4 cups of water
5 cloves of garlic, chopped
2 teaspoons herbs
5 tablespoons Olive oil
salt and pepper
1 bunch of dill, chopped

How to Cook:

1. Preheat the oven to 250°-270° Fahrenheit. Cut the baguette or white bread into the small cubes and toss them with the salt, pepper and herbs. Place the baguette cubes on a baking sheet. Bake the croutons for about 10-15 minutes until golden brown and crispy.
2. In a pot, heat the Olive oil and fry the chopped onions with the garlic for about for 5-10 minutes until clear and caramelized. Then mix in the salmon, salt and pepper. Pour the meat broth and boil it covered for about 15-20 minutes.
3. After 20 minutes add in the pumpkin and all the remaining ingredients. Then reduce the heat and

continue to boil for around 20 minutes but don't forget to skim the foam from the soup.

4. Spoon the croutons and sprinkle the chopped dill on top. Portion the soup into bowls or mugs and serve with the cream and bread!

Nutritional Information:
Calories: 227; Total fat: 48 oz; Total carbohydrates: 60 oz; Protein: 39 oz

Spicy Tomatoes-Salmon Soup

Prep Time: 15 min. | Cooking Time: 60 min. | Servings: 2

Ingredients:

25 oz salmon, cubed
10 medium tomatoes, diced
4 onions, peeled and chopped
1 baguette or white bread
2 cups of vegetable broth
4 cups of water
5 cloves of garlic, chopped
2 teaspoons herbs
5 tablespoons Olive oil
1 teaspoon chili pepper powder
salt and pepper
1 bunch of basil, chopped

How to Cook:

1. Preheat the oven to 250°-270° Fahrenheit. Cut the baguette or white bread into the small cubes and toss them with the salt, pepper and herbs. Place the baguette cubes on a baking sheet. Bake the croutons for about 10-15 minutes until golden brown and crispy.
2. Whip up the tomatoes using a blender until there is a smooth and creamy consistency and homogenous mass.
3. In a pot, heat the Olive oil and fry the chopped onions with the garlic for about for 5-10 minutes until clear and caramelized. Then mix in the salmon, salt and pepper. Pour the meat broth and boil the soup covered for about 15-20 minutes.
4. After 20 minutes add in the whipped tomatoes and all the remaining ingredients. Then reduce the heat and continue to boil for around 20 minutes but don't forget to skim the foam from the soup.
5. Spoon the croutons and top with the basil. Portion the soup into bowls or mugs and serve with the cream and bread!

Nutritional Information:
Calories: 227; Total fat: 48 oz; Total carbohydrates: 56 oz; Protein: 36 oz

Salmon Soup with Eggplants and Cream

Prep Time: 20 min. | *Cooking Time: 40 min.* | *Servings: 4*

Ingredients:

20 oz salmon, diced
2 eggplants
4 potatoes, peeled and diced
2 onions, peeled and chopped
4 chopped garlic cloves
1 cup of cream
10 oz unsalted butter
5 tablespoons white flour
2 carrots, peeled and chopped
2 tablespoons soy sauce
2 tablespoons sunflower oil
1 teaspoon sea salt
1 teaspoon pepper
Herbs de Provence

How to Cook:

1. Let's trim off the top and bottom of the eggplants. Don't peel away the eggplants skin. Then cut it into small cubes and sprinkle eggplant cubes with sea salt and pepper.

2. In a skillet or wok, melt the unsalted butter and fry the onions for around 10 minutes until clear and caramelized and then add in the eggplants, flour and cream to stew for the few minutes on a low heat.

3. In a pot, heat the water and add in all the vegetables and the butter-cream mixture. Then reduce the heat and continue to boil for around 30 minutes but don't forget to skim the foam from the soup.
4. Add in the salt and pepper. Portion the salmon and eggplants soup into two bowls or mugs and dollop each bowl with the Herbs de Provence. Serve the soup with the wheat bread! Remember that this dish should be served warm.

Nutritional Information:
Calories: 261; Total fat: 48 oz; Total carbohydrates: 55 oz; Protein: 34 oz

Salmon Heads and Bell Peppers Soup

Prep Time: 20 min. | Cooking Time: 65 min. | Servings: 4

Ingredients:

4 medium salmon heads
4 medium and red bell peppers, diced
4 medium and orange bell peppers, diced
4 potatoes, peeled and diced
2 onions, peeled and chopped
5 oz white bread, cubed
4 chopped garlic cloves
10 oz unsalted butter
5 tablespoons white flour
2 carrots, peeled and chopped
2 tablespoons soy sauce
2 tablespoons sunflower oil
salt and pepper
Herbs de Provence

How to Cook:

1. In a pot, boil the salmon heads for around 20 minutes. Add in some salt. Remove the foam from the salmon heads soup.
2. In a skillet or wok, melt the unsalted butter and fry the onions for around 10 minutes until clear and caramelized and then add in the flour and cream to stew for the few minutes on a low heat.
3. In a pot with the salmon heads, combine all the vegetables and the butter-onions mixture. Reduce the heat and continue to boil for around 30 minutes

but don't forget to skim the foam from the salmon soup.

4. Meanwhile, preheat the oven to 240°-260° Fahrenheit. Cut the white bread into the small cubes and toss them with the salt, pepper and herbs. Place the bread cubes on a baking sheet. Bake the croutons for about 10-15 minutes until golden brown and crispy.

5. Portion the salmon heads and bell peppers soup into four bowls or mugs and dollop each bowl with the herbs. Serve the soup with the wheat bread! Remember that this dish should be served warm.

Nutritional Information:

Calories: 252; Total fat: 53 oz; Total carbohydrates: 60 oz; Protein: 38 oz

Salmon Bouillon with Noodles and Vegetables

***Prep Time: 10 min. | Cooking Time: 50
min. | Servings: 4***

Ingredients:

25 oz salmon, cubed
1 cup of small noodles
5 garlic cloves, chopped
2 onions, peeled and chopped
2 carrots, peeled and chopped
1 celery, chopped
2 tablespoons garlic powder
salt and pepper

How to Prepare:

1. In a bowl, combine the pepper, garlic powder, chopped garlic and some salt. Season the salmon

with the pepper, and toss in the garlic powder, salt, and garlic. Set the salmon aside to marinate the fish for at least 5 hours unrefrigerated at room temperature or place in the fridge overnight.

2. Place the salmon into the saucepan and add in all the ingredients except for the onions and then boil for about 40 minutes. Don't forget to skim the foam from the bouillon.

3. Meanwhile, heat the oil and fry the onions over medium heat for around 10 minutes until caramelized and clear.

4. 10 minutes before the bouillon is ready mix in the onions and boil with the lid closed.

5. Portion the salmon, noodles and vegetables bouillon into four bowls or mugs and dollop each bowl with the cream and chopped chives. Serve the salmon and vegetables bouillon with the bread, and wine.

Nutritional Information:

Calories: 218; Total fat: 28 oz; Total carbohydrates: 34 oz;

Protein: 15 oz

Salmon Heads Bouillon with Croutons and Garlic

Prep Time: 10 min. | Cooking Time: 50 min. | Servings: 4

Ingredients:

4 big salmon heads
1 baguette
8 garlic cloves, minced
2 carrots, peeled and chopped
1 celery, chopped
2 tablespoons sunflower oil
2 tablespoons garlic powder
2 tablespoons kosher salt
1 tablespoon herbs

How to Prepare:

1. Preheat the oven to 250°-270° Fahrenheit. Cut the baguette or white bread into the small cubes and toss them with the 1 tablespoon kosher or sea salt and herbs. Place the baguette cubes on a baking sheet. Bake the croutons for about 10-15 minutes until golden brown and crispy.
2. In a bowl, combine the garlic powder, minced garlic and some salt. Toss the salmon heads in the garlic and salt. Set the salmon heads aside to marinate for at least 2 hours unrefrigerated at room temperature.
3. Place the salmon heads into the saucepan and add in all the remaining ingredients and then boil for about 40 minutes. Don't forget to skim the foam from the bouillon.

4. Portion the salmon heads bouillon into four bowls or mugs and dollop each bowl with the croutons. Serve the salmon and vegetables bouillon with the croutons and wine.

Nutritional Information:

Calories: 216; Total fat: 27 oz; Total carbohydrates: 34 oz;

Protein: 15 oz

Zucchini Noodles and Salmon Soup with Basil

Prep Time: 10 min. | Cooking Time: 50 min. | Servings: 4

Ingredients:

5 salmon heads
1 zucchini, peeled and spiralized
10 basil leaves, chopped
8 garlic cloves, chopped
2 onions, peeled and chopped
2 carrots, peeled and chopped
1 teaspoon powdered Chili pepper
2 teaspoons powdered garlic
1 teaspoon nutmeg
salt and pepper

How to Prepare:

1. In a bowl, combine the powdered chili pepper, powdered garlic, nutmeg, chopped garlic, some salt, and pepper. Season the salmon heads with the salt and pepper, and toss in the powdered garlic, powdered Chili pepper, garlic, and nutmeg mix. Set the salmon heads aside. Marinate the salmon heads for at least 5 hours unrefrigerated at room temperature.
2. Place the salmon heads into the saucepan and add in all the ingredients except for the spiralized zucchini and basil leaves. Boil for about 50 minutes. Don't forget to skim the foam from the soup.
3. 10 minutes before the soup is ready mix in the zucchini noodles and boil with the lid closed until the zucchini is soft.

4. Serve the spicy zucchini noodles and salmon soup warm with the cream and wine.

Nutritional Information:
Calories: 221; Total fat: 27 oz; Total carbohydrates: 38 oz; Protein: 22 oz

Salmon-Carrots Cream Soup with Chives and Ginger

Prep Time: 15 min. | Cooking Time: 65 min. | Servings: 2

Ingredients:

25 oz salmon, cubed
10 medium carrots
1 teaspoon ginger grated or powder
4 onions, peeled and chopped
1 baguette
2 cups of vegetable broth
4 cups of water
1 cup of cream
5 cloves of garlic, chopped
2 teaspoons herbs
5 tablespoons Olive oil
salt and pepper

How to Cook:

1. Preheat the oven to 250°-270° Fahrenheit. Cut the baguette or white bread into the small cubes and toss them with the salt, pepper and herbs. Place the baguette cubes on a baking sheet. Bake the croutons for about 10-15 minutes until golden brown and crispy. Meanwhile, boil the carrots until soft.
2. Whip up the carrots using a blender until there is a smooth and creamy consistency and homogenous mass.
3. In a pot, heat the Olive oil and fry the chopped onions with the garlic for about for 5-10 minutes until clear and caramelized. Then mix in the salmon, salt and pepper. Pour the meat broth and boil the soup covered for about 15-20 minutes.
4. After 20 minutes add in the whipped carrots and all the remaining ingredients. Then reduce the heat and continue to boil for around 20 minutes but don't forget to skim the foam from the soup.
5. Spoon the croutons and top with the chopped chives. Portion the soup into bowls or mugs and serve!

Nutritional Information:
Calories: 223; Total fat: 42 oz; Total carbohydrates: 57 oz; Protein: 38 oz

Salmon-Ginger Soup

Prep Time: 15 min. | *Cooking Time: 40 min.* | *Servings: 4*

Ingredients:

20 oz salmon, diced
1 teaspoon ginger, grated or powder
4 potatoes, peeled and diced
2 onions, peeled and chopped
4 chopped garlic cloves
2 tablespoons soy sauce
2 tablespoons Olive oil
salt and pepper

How to Cook:

1. In a skillet or wok, heat the oil and fry the onions for around 10 minutes until clear and caramelized.
2. In a pot, heat the water and add in all the vegetables and salmon. Then reduce the heat and continue to boil for around 30 minutes but don't forget to skim the foam from the soup.
3. Add in the salt and pepper. Portion the salmon-ginger soup into four bowls or mugs. Serve the soup with the wheat bread. Remember that this dish should be served warm.

Nutritional Information:

Calories: 247; Total fat: 61 oz; Total carbohydrates: 57 oz; Protein: 32 oz

Salmon Soup with Spanish Herbs

Prep Time: 15 min. | Cooking Time: 40 min. | Servings: 4

Ingredients:

20 oz salmon, cubed
1 teaspoon Pimentón – dried Paprika or Spanish paprika, or pimentón
1 teaspoon Azafrán - Saffron
1 teaspoon Perejil, dried Parsley
1 teaspoon Guindilla - Cayenne Pepper
Laurel (Bay Leaf)
4 potatoes, peeled and diced
2 medium onions, peeled and chopped
2 carrots, peeled and diced
4 chopped garlic cloves
2 tablespoons soy sauce
2 tablespoons Olive oil
0.5 teaspoon nutmeg
salt and pepper
greenery, chopped

How to Cook:

1. In a bowl, combine garlic, nutmeg some salt and pepper. Season the cubed salmon with the spices mix. Set the salmon cubes aside to marinate them for at least 1 hour unrefrigerated at room temperature or place in the fridge for few hours.
2. In a skillet or wok, heat the oil and fry the onions for around 10 minutes until clear and caramelized.
3. In a pot, heat the water and add in all the vegetables, Spanish herbs and salmon. Then reduce

the heat and continue to boil for around 30 minutes but don't forget to skim the foam from the soup.

4. Add in the salt and pepper. Portion the salmon soup into four bowls or mugs and dollop each bowl with the chopped greenery. Serve the soup with the white bread! Remember that this dish should be served warm.

Nutritional Information:

Calories: 250; Total fat: 62 oz; Total carbohydrates: 55 oz; Protein: 37 oz

Salmon in Wine with Vegetables Salad and Cashews

Prep Time: 15 min. | Cooking Time: 30 min. | Servings: 3

Ingredients:

30 oz salmon fillet, cut into pieces
2 glasses of red wine
1 cup of cashews
4 tomatoes cut into rings
1 tablespoon lemon juice
2 tablespoons powdered garlic
5 cloves of garlic, chopped
3 tablespoons Olive oil
3 tablespoons butter, melted
2 tablespoons Herbs de Provence
salt and pepper

Salad Ingredients:

   5 oz lettuce, chopped
   5 teaspoons soy sauce
   2 tomatoes, sliced
   2 onions, peeled and sliced

How to Cook:

1. Preheat the oven to 250°-270°Fahrenheit and roast the cashews in the oven for 10 minutes until lightly browned and crispy and then set aside to cool completely. Then grind the cashews using a food processor or blender.
2. In a bowl, combine powdered garlic, garlic, some salt, and pepper. Season the salmon with the Herbs de Provence, salt, pepper and garlic mix, and toss in the melted butter. Pour the white wine on top and marinate the salmon for at least 1 hour but no longer than 2 hours unrefrigerated at room temperature or in the fridge.
3. Heat the grill and place the salmon on grill (skin down). Cover the salmon and grill for around 10-20 minutes brushing with the Olive oil or marinade.
4. 10 minutes before the salmon is ready place the few tomatoes on grill.
5. Combine all the salad ingredients and mix well.
6. Sprinkle the cashews and lemon juice over the salmon and salad and serve with the cold beer.

Nutritional Information:

Calories: 303; Total fat: 47 oz; Total carbohydrates: 56 oz; Protein: 37 oz

Salmon with Tuna, Oranges and Herbs

Prep Time: 20 min. | Cooking Time: 40-50 min. | Servings: 4

Ingredients:

30 oz salmon, cubed
1 can of tuna
1 cup of cashews
2 cups of oranges, peeled and cubed
4 onions, peeled and chopped
5 tablespoons Olive oil
5 tablespoons freshly squeezed lemon juice
1 teaspoon powdered red pepper
2 tablespoons powdered garlic
2 teaspoons Herbs de Provence
1 teaspoon nutmeg, ground
salt and pepper

How to Prepare:

1. In a bowl, mash the tuna with the fork.
2. Preheat the oven to 250°-270°Fahrenheit and roast the cashews in the oven for 10 minutes until lightly browned and crispy and then set aside to cool completely. Then grind the cashews using a food processor or blender.
3. In a bowl, combine Herbs de Provence, powdered red pepper, powdered garlic, nutmeg, and some salt. Season the cubed salmon with the salt and pepper, and toss in the powdered garlic, powdered red pepper, and nutmeg mix. Set the salmon cubes aside to marinate them for at least 1 hour unrefrigerated at room temperature or place in the fridge for few hours.

4. Preheat the oven to 300°-340° Fahrenheit, and bake the salmon and tuna for around 40-50 minutes until golden brown and crispy. Toss the pumpkin in the Olive oil and salt. 10 minutes before the salmon is ready add in the onions and oranges and bake them with the salmon cubes.
5. Spoon the cashews over the salmon and tuna.
6. Sprinkle the salt and pepper and pour the freshly squeezed lemon juice over the salmon and you are free to serve the fish cubes in separate dishes with a white wine. Remember that this dish should be served warm.

Nutritional Information:
Calories: 315; Total fat: 57 oz; Total carbohydrates: 76 oz; Protein: 35 oz

Baked Salmon with Buckwheat and Feta Cheese

Prep Time: 20 min.│Cooking Time: 60 min.│Servings: 4

Ingredients:
4 salmon fillets
2 cups of buckwheat
2 onions, peeled and chopped
4 carrots, peeled and diced
4 tomatoes, sliced
20 oz Feta cheese, crumbled
6 tablespoons Olive oil
10 fresh basil leaves
salt and pepper

How to Prepare:

1. Boil the water to cook the buckwheat for 15-20 minutes until half-cooked.
2. In a frying pan or wok, heat the Olive oil and fry the onions and carrots for 5-10 minutes on medium heat until clear and caramelized.
3. Preheat the oven to 320°-340° Fahrenheit and bake the salmon and buckwheat with the carrots, onions, salt and pepper for 30 minutes until the vegetables are soft.
4. 5 minutes before the salmon and buckwheat are ready open the oven and place the sliced tomatoes and the crumbled Feta cheese on top.
5. Portion the salmon into plates and dollop each plate with the basil and tomatoes. Remember that this dish should be served warm.

Nutritional Information:

Calories: 320; Total fat: 45 oz; Total carbohydrates: 68 oz; Protein: 38 oz

Salmon with Veal, Chives and Onions

Prep Time: 20 min. | Cooking Time: 40-50 min. | Servings: 2

Ingredients:
20 oz salmon fillets, cubed
15 oz veal, cubed
2 bunches of green and fresh chives, chopped
1 cup of cashews
7 medium onions, peeled and chopped
1 zucchini, peeled and cubed
5 tablespoons Olive oil
5 tablespoons freshly squeezed lemon juice
1 teaspoon powdered red pepper
2 tablespoons powdered garlic
1 teaspoon nutmeg, ground
salt and pepper

How to Prepare:

1. Preheat the oven to 200°-230° Fahrenheit and roast the cashews in the oven for 10 minutes until lightly browned and crispy and then set aside to cool completely. Then grind the cashews using a food processor or blender.

2. In a bowl, combine powdered red pepper, powdered garlic, nutmeg, chopped onions and some salt. Season the cubed salmon fillets and veal with the salt and pepper, and toss in the powdered garlic, powdered red pepper, onions, and nutmeg mix. Set the salmon and veal cubes aside to marinate them for at least 1 hour unrefrigerated at room temperature or place in the fridge for few hours.

3. Preheat the oven to 320°-360° Fahrenheit, and bake the veal for around 20-30 minutes until golden brown and crispy. Then add in the salmon and bake for 20 minutes further. 10 minutes before the salmon and veal are ready add in the zucchini and chives, and bake them with the salmon and veal cubes.

4. Spoon the cashews over the zucchini, onions, fish and veal cubes. Sprinkle the salt and pepper and pour the freshly squeezed lemon juice over the fish and veal and you are free to serve the salmon- veal cubes with the vegetables and nuts in separate dishes with a white wine. Remember that this dish should be served warm.

Nutritional Information:

Calories: 394; Total fat: 54 oz; Total carbohydrates: 75 oz; Protein: 42 oz

Spicy Grilled Salmon in Lemon Juice

Prep Time: 10 min. | Cooking Time: 20 min. | Servings: 3

Ingredients:

30 oz salmon fillet, cut into cubes
2 big lemons
2 tablespoons powdered garlic
2 tablespoons Herbs de Provence
1 tablespoon chili pepper powder
1 teaspoon salt
1 teaspoon pepper

How to Cook:

1. In a bowl, combine the spices: powdered garlic, herbs, salt, pepper and chili pepper powder. Mix the spices well. Place the salmon cubes on the cutting board. Sprinkle the salmon cubes with the powdered garlic, Herbs de Provence, salt, pepper and chili pepper powder mix. Sprinkle the salmon cubes on all sides.
2. Place the salmon in a bowl. Halve the lemons and then squeeze the fruits.
3. Pour the lemon juices over the salmon cubes and marinate the salmon for at least 1 hour but no longer than 2 hours unrefrigerated at room temperature or in the fridge.
4. Heat the grill and place the salmon on grill (skin down). Grill the salmon for around 10-20 minutes brushing with the spices and fruits marinade.

5. Portion the salmon into the few plates or bowls and dollop each plate with the vegetables salad. Remember that this grilled salmon should be served warm. Serve with the cold beer.

Nutritional Information:

Calories: 305; Total fat: 51 oz; Total carbohydrates: 59 oz; Protein: 42 oz

Spicy Grilled Salmon in White Wine with Quinoa

Prep Time: 15 min. | Cooking Time: 50 min. | Servings: 3

Ingredients:

30 oz salmon fillet, cut into cubes
2 cups of white wine
2 limes
1 cup of quinoa
2 cups of vegetable broth
1 tablespoon Olive oil
2 tablespoons powdered garlic
2 tablespoons nutmeg
1 tablespoon chili pepper powder
1 teaspoon salt
1 teaspoon pepper

How to Cook:

1. Boil the quinoa in the vegetable broth for around 20-30 minutes or follow the cooking time suggested on the packet. Add 1 tablespoon olive oil.

2. In a bowl, combine the spices: powdered garlic, nutmeg, salt, pepper and chili pepper powder. Mix the spices well. Place the salmon cubes on the cutting board. Sprinkle the salmon cubes with the powdered garlic, nutmeg, salt, pepper and chili pepper powder mix. Sprinkle the salmon cubes on all sides.

3. Place the salmon in a bowl. Halve the limes and then squeeze them.

4. Pour the white wine and lime juice over the salmon cubes and marinate the salmon for at least 1 hour but no longer than 2 hours unrefrigerated at room temperature or in the fridge.
5. Heat the grill and place the salmon on grill (skin down). Grill the salmon for around 10-20 minutes brushing with the spices and white wine marinade.
6. Portion the salmon into the few plates or bowls and dollop each plate with the quinoa. Remember that this grilled salmon should be served warm.

Nutritional Information:

Calories: 305; Total fat: 51 oz; Total carbohydrates: 58 oz; Protein: 42 oz

Salmon with Couscous and Parsley

Prep Time: 20 min. | Cooking Time: 60 minutes | Servings: 5

Ingredients:
1 lb salmon, cubed
2 cups of couscous
2 bunches of fresh parsley, chopped
3 cups vegetable broth
2 onions, peeled and chopped
4 cloves of garlic, minced
1 cauliflower, cubed
20 oz cherry tomatoes, halved
3 carrots, peeled and grated
5 oz Gouda cheese, crumbled
7 tablespoons sesame seeds oil
2 teaspoons turmeric, ground
2 teaspoons Cayenne pepper, ground
salt and pepper

How to Prepare:

1. Boil the couscous in the vegetable broth for around 20 minutes or follow the cooking time suggested on the packet. Add 1 tablespoon sesame seeds oil. In parallel, boil the cauliflower to half-cooked.
2. In a frying pan or wok, heat the oil and fry the salmon for around 20 minutes on medium heat until golden brown and then add in the onions, carrots, garlic salt and pepper. Stew for 10 minutes with the lid closed.
3. In a frying pan, combine the couscous with the salmon, vegetables, turmeric, Cayenne pepper and sprinkle sesame seeds oil with chopped chives on top.
4. Add in the Gouda cheese and chopped parsley. Close the lid and stew for 10 minutes to melt the cheese.
5. Portion the salmon and couscous into two plates and sprinkle each plate with the lemon juice. Serve with the marinated tomatoes or cucumbers. Remember that this dish should be served warm.

Nutritional Information:

Calories: 316; Total fat: 35 oz; Total carbohydrates: 53 oz; Protein: 33 oz

Salmon with Sweet Potatoes and Pineapples

Prep Time: 20 min. | Cooking Time: 40-50 min. | Servings: 4

Ingredients:

30 oz salmon fillets, cubed
2 cups of pineapples, cubed
7 medium sweet potatoes, peeled and halved
5 tablespoons Olive oil
5 tablespoons freshly squeezed lemon juice
1 teaspoon powdered red pepper
2 tablespoons powdered garlic
1 teaspoon nutmeg, ground
salt and pepper

How to Prepare:

1. In a bowl, combine the powdered red pepper, powdered garlic, nutmeg, and some salt. Season the salmon fillets with the salt and pepper, and toss in the powdered garlic, powdered red pepper, and nutmeg mix. Set the salmon fillets aside to marinate them for at least 1 hour unrefrigerated at room temperature or place in the fridge for few hours.
2. Toss the sweet potatoes and pineapple cubes in the Olive oil and salt.
3. Preheat the oven to 300°-340° Fahrenheit and bake the salmon for around 40-50 minutes until golden brown and crispy. Then bake the sweet potatoes and pineapples with the salmon cubes.

4. Sprinkle the salt and pepper and pour the freshly squeezed lemon juice over the salmon and you are free to serve the salmon cubes with the sweet potatoes and pineapple cubes in separate dishes with a white wine. Remember that this dish should be served warm.

Nutritional Information:
Calories: 297; Total fat: 55 oz; Total carbohydrates: 78 oz; Protein: 36 oz

Salmon and Cuscus

Prep Time: 10 min. | Cooking Time: 35 min. | Servings: 2

Ingredients:

2 cans salmon
2 cups of cuscus
2 eggs
3 cups vegetable broth
5 tomatoes, halved
1 tablespoon Olive oil
1 teaspoon nutmeg
Sea salt, to taste
Pepper, to taste
1 small lemon

How to Prepare:

1. Boil the cuscus in the vegetable broth for around 20 minutes or follow the cooking time suggested on the packet. Add 1 tablespoon Olive oil. In parallel, mash the salmon with the fork or potato masher.
2. Heat the water and boil the eggs. Then chop them.
3. In a frying pan, combine the cuscus with the salmon, eggs, tomatoes, nutmeg, sea salt and pepper. Fry the mix on a low heat for 15 minutes.
4. Meanwhile, halve the lemon and then squeeze it.
5. Portion the salmon and cuscus into two plates and sprinkle each plate with the lemon juice. Remember that this dish should be served warm.

Nutritional Information:

Calories: 315; Total fat: 34 oz; Total carbohydrates: 54 oz; Protein: 36 oz

Kippered Salmon with Dill

Prep Time: 20 min. | *Servings: 2*

Ingredients:
2 salmon fillets, sliced
2-3 teaspoons Sea salt
2 lemons
2 tablespoons powdered garlic
1 teaspoon nutmeg, ground
1 tablespoon Herbs de Provence
1 bunch of dill, chopped

How to Prepare:

1. In a bowl, combine the spices: powdered garlic, nutmeg, Herbs de Provence, salt and dill. Mix the spices well. Sprinkle the salmon slices with the powdered garlic, nutmeg, salt, pepper, herbs and dill mix. Sprinkle the salmon slices on all sides.

2. Place the salmon in the plastic kitchen storage container. Halve the lemons and then squeeze them.
3. Pour the lemon juice over the salmon slices and marinate the salmon for at least 20 hours in the fridge.
4. Eat the salmon with the sliced baguette or white bread, garlic butter and parsley.

Nutritional Information:
Calories: 187; Total fat: 43 oz; Total carbohydrates: 61 oz; Protein: 32 oz

Spicy Kippered Salmon wit Parsley

Prep Time: 20 min. | Servings: 2

Ingredients:
2 salmon fillets, sliced
2-3 teaspoons Sea salt
2 teaspoons chili pepper powder
1 teaspoon black pepper
2 lemons
0.5 teaspoon oregano
1 bunch of parsley, chopped

How to Prepare:
1. In a bowl, combine the spices: sea salt, chili pepper, black pepper, oregano and parsley. Mix the spices well. Sprinkle the salmon slices with the sea salt, chili pepper, black pepper, oregano and parsley. Sprinkle the salmon slices on all sides.
2. Place the salmon into the plastic kitchen storage container. Halve the lemons and then squeeze them.
3. Pour the lemon juice over the salmon slices and marinate the salmon for at least 20-24 hours in the fridge.
4. Eat the salmon with the sliced baguette or white bread, butter and chives.

Nutritional Information:
Calories: 192; Total fat: 41 oz; Total carbohydrates: 59 oz; Protein: 31 oz

Salmon in Foil with Amaranth and Avocado Sauce

Prep Time: 20 min. | *Cooking Time: 1 hour* | *Servings: 4*

Ingredients:
4 salmon fillets
2 cups of amaranth
1 avocado, peeled and cubed
1 fresh cucumber, sliced
4 garlic cloves, minced
5 tablespoons Olive oil
2 teaspoons chili powder
2 lemons
salt and pepper
Herbs de Provence
5 fresh basil leaves, chopped

How to Cook:

1. Boil the water to cook the amaranth for 25 minutes or follow the cooking time suggested on the packet. Add 2 tablespoons Olive oil when the amaranth is ready.
2. Halve the lemons and then squeeze them. Pour the lemon juice over the salmon fillets and marinate the salmon fillets in herbs and lemon juice for 5 hours.
3. Wrap the fish fillets in foil. Preheat the oven to 300°-340° Fahrenheit, and bake the salmon fillets in foil for around 40 minutes until golden brown and crispy.
4. Let's get to the sauce now – blend the avocado with the garlic cloves, chili powder, salt and pepper using a blender.

5. Pour some squeezed lemon juice and mix well. The avocado sauce is ready!
6. Pour the avocado sauce over the salmon fillets. Serve the salmon fillets with the amaranth, avocado sauce and cucumbers and sprinkle the basil on top to garnish.

Nutritional Information:

Calories: 284; Total fat: 56 oz; Total carbohydrates: 65 oz; Protein: 40 oz

Salmon in Orange Juice with Walnuts and Sesame Seeds

Prep Time: 25 min. | Cooking Time: 60 min. | Servings: 2

Ingredients:
8 salmon slices
1 cup of walnuts
4 tablespoons sesame seeds
2 big oranges
5 tablespoons Olive oil
5 teaspoons herbs
1 teaspoon nutmeg, ground
Sea salt, to taste
Black pepper, to taste
2 tablespoons soy sauce
2 teaspoon sesame seeds
5 oz chives, chopped

How to Prepare:

1. Preheat the oven to 250°-270°Fahrenheit and roast the walnuts in the oven for 10 minutes until lightly browned and crispy and then set aside to cool completely. Then grind the walnuts using a food processor or blender.

2. In a bowl, combine herbs, nutmeg, and some salt. Season the salmon with the herbs, nutmeg and salt. Halve the oranges and then squeeze them. Pour the orange juice over the salmon slices and marinate the salmon in herbs and orange juice for at least 5 hours unrefrigerated at room temperature or place in the fridge overnight.

3. Preheat the oven to 330°-350° Fahrenheit, and bake the salmon in foil with walnuts for around 30-40 minutes until golden brown.

4. Sprinkle the salt and pepper and pour the soy sauce over the salmon. Portion the salmon into two plates and dollop each plate with the chives and sesame seeds. Now you are free to serve the fish in separate dishes with a white wine. Remember that this dish should be served warm.

Nutritional Information:

Calories: 258; Total fat: 54 oz; Total carbohydrates: 67 oz; Protein: 39 oz

Salmon Cutlets with Quinoa

Prep Time: 10 min. | Cooking Time: 55 min. | Servings: 3

Ingredients:

20 oz salmon, ground
2 cups of quinoa
2 eggs
2 tablespoons oats
3 tablespoons Olive oil
1 teaspoon nutmeg
Sea salt, to taste
Pepper, to taste
1 small lemon
1 teaspoon soy sauce

How to Prepare:

1. Boil the quinoa in the water for around 20 minutes or follow the cooking time suggested on the packet. Add 1 tablespoon Olive oil.
2. Soak the oats in the warm water for 15 minutes and then drain them.
3. In parallel, combine the ground salmon with the eggs, nutmeg, salt and pepper and mash the ingredients well using the fork.
4. Halve the lemon and then squeeze it. Pour the lemon juice over the ground salmon and mix well. Marinate the salmon in spices and lemon juice for at least 5 hours unrefrigerated at room temperature or place in the fridge overnight.

5. Form the palm-sized salmon cutlets out of the ground salmon fish. Place the salmon cutlets into your skillet.
6. In a skillet, heat the olive oil and stew the salmon cutlets on a low heat for 35 minutes with the lid closed
7. Portion the salmon cutlets and quinoa into plates or bowls and sprinkle each plate with the soy sauce. Remember that this dish should be served warm.

Nutritional Information:
Calories: 315; Total fat: 38 oz; Total carbohydrates: 57 oz; Protein: 35 oz

Salmon Cutlets with Cashews and Cuscus

Prep Time: 10 min. | Cooking Time: 70 min. | Servings: 3

Ingredients:
20 oz salmon, ground
1 cup of cashews
1 cup of cuscus
2 eggs
3 tablespoons Olive oil
1 teaspoon nutmeg
Sea salt, to taste
Pepper, to taste
1 small lemon
1 teaspoon soy sauce

How to Prepare:

1. Preheat the oven to 200°-230°Fahrenheit and roast the cashews in the oven for 10 minutes until lightly browned and crispy and then set aside to cool completely. Then grind the cashews using a food processor or blender.
2. Wash the cuscus several times. Boil the cuscus for around 20 minutes or follow the cooking time suggested on the packet. Add 1 tablespoon Olive oil.
3. In parallel, combine the ground salmon with the eggs, cashews, nutmeg, salt and pepper and mash them well using the fork.
4. Halve the lemon and then squeeze it. Pour the lemon juice over the ground salmon and marinate the salmon in spices and lemon juice for at least 5

hours unrefrigerated at room temperature or place in the fridge overnight.

5. Form the palm-sized salmon cutlets out of the ground fish.
6. Preheat the oven to 330°-350° Fahrenheit, and bake the salmon cutlets for around 30-40 minutes until golden brown.
7. Portion the salmon cutlets and cuscus into plates or bowls and sprinkle each plate with the soy sauce. Remember that this dish should be served warm.

Nutritional Information:
Calories: 318; Total fat: 38 oz; Total carbohydrates: 64 oz; Protein: 38 oz

Salmon with Broccoli, Peas and Noodles

Prep Time: 25 min. | Cooking Time: 55 min. | Servings: 4

Ingredients:

30 oz salmon, diced
any type of noodles (around 20 oz)
1 can of marinated field peas
1 medium fresh broccoli
10 cloves of garlic, minced
1 cup of cream
2 onions, peeled and chopped
4 fresh cherry tomatoes, halved
5 tablespoons white flour
5 tablespoons mayonnaise
Olive oil
salt and pepper
oregano

How to Cook:

1. Boil the water and cook the noodles for around 15 minutes or follow the cooking time suggested on the packet. Add 1 tablespoon Olive oil. In parallel, boil the broccoli to half-cooked.
2. In a skillet, heat the oil and fry the onions for 5-10 minutes until clear and caramelized.
3. In the same oil with onions and salmon, fry the garlic for 5 minutes. (on a medium heat).
4. Add in the white flour, cream, mayonnaise and stir well. Boil the sauce, stirring over medium heat for around 5 min. Add in the oregano, salt and the pepper and close the lid to leave for 5 minutes, so that the sauce absorbs the flour.
5. Heat the oil and fry the salmon and broccoli for 15-20 minutes.
6. Place the salmon, broccoli and noodles into the plates or bowls and dollop each bowl with the sauce and marinated peas. Then mix well.
7. Halve the tomatoes and place them on a plate with the salmon and noodles. Now you are free to serve your fish with the white wine!

Nutritional Information:

Calories: 319; Total fat: 55 oz; Total carbohydrates: 67 oz; Protein: 35 oz

Salmon, Tomatoes and Garlic Pasta with Romano Cheese

Prep Time: 25 min. | Cooking Time: 85 min. | Servings: 4

Ingredients:

40 oz salmon, diced
any type of pasta (around 15 oz)
5 medium tomatoes, diced
2 tablespoons garlic butter
10 oz fresh basil leaves, chopped
7 oz rye bread
1 teaspoon herbs
2 onions, peeled and chopped
1 garlic clove, chopped
4 tablespoons white flour
1 cup of milk or cream
7 tablespoons sunflower oil
5 oz Romano cheese
1 cup of white wine
salt and pepper
Herbs de Provence

How to Cook:

1. Boil the water and cook the pasta for 20 minutes. (or follow the cooking time suggested on the packet). Add 2 tablespoons garlic butter when the pasta is cooked. Later we will use the water from the boiled pasta.

2. Cut the rye bread into the small cubes and toss them with the salt and herbs. Preheat the oven to 250°-

270° Fahrenheit and spread the rye bread cubes on a baking sheet. Bake the croutons for about 10-15 minutes until golden brown and crispy.

3. In a skillet, heat the oil and fry the salmon for 15-20 minutes. Then mix in the onions, basil and chopped garlic and fry for 10 minutes.

4. Spoon the flour, pour the water from the boiled pasta and white wine and cook for 10 min.

5. Next pour the milk or cream and stew for 10 min with the lid closed.

6. Spoon the pasta into the salmon and sauce and add in Herbs de Provence, some salt and pepper and stir well.

7. Grate the Romano cheese on top and add the rye bread croutons. Serve the salmon pasta with the white wine!

Nutritional Information:
Calories: 326; Total fat: 53 oz; Total carbohydrates: 68 oz; Protein: 34 oz

Baked Salmon with Sweet Potatoes, Herbs, Plums and Romano Cheese

---

Prep Time: 20 min. | Cooking Time: 50 min. | Servings: 2

Ingredients:

5 salmon fillets
10 medium sweet potatoes, peeled and cubed
8 oz (1 pack) Romano cheese, grated
4 plums, pitted and cubed
2 red onions, peeled and chopped
4 tablespoons Olive oil
4 tablespoons lemon juice
2 tablespoons herbs (rosemary and marjoram)
salt and pepper

How to Prepare:

1. Preheat the oven to 310°-330° Fahrenheit and bake the salmon fillets with the sweet potatoes, plums, onions, Olive oil, herbs, salt and pepper for 50 minutes until the potatoes are golden brown crispy.
2. 10 minutes before the salmon and vegetables are ready open the oven and sprinkle the grated Romano cheese on top.
3. Portion the salmon into two plates and dollop each plate with the lemon juice. Remember that this dish should be served warm.

Nutritional Information:

Calories: 321; Total fat: 38 oz; Total carbohydrates: 53 oz; Protein: 33 oz

Salmon Balls with Oregano and Lemon

Prep Time: 15 min. | Cooking Time: 40 min. | Servings: 4

Ingredients:
30 oz salmon stuffing (ground salmon)
2 teaspoons oregano
5 tablespoons Olive oil
2 medium lemons
2 tablespoons powdered garlic
1 teaspoon Herbs de Provence
salt and pepper
dill, chopped

How to Prepare:
1. In a bowl, combine the salmon stuffing with the oregano, powdered garlic, Herbs de Provence, pepper and some salt. Mix well.

2. Form the salmon balls out of the ground fish mixture. Spoon the salmon balls into your baking pan.
3. Preheat the oven to 320°-360° Fahrenheit, and bake the salmon balls for around 30-40 minutes until golden brown.
4. Halve the lemons and then squeeze the fruits.
5. Sprinkle the salt and pepper and pour the freshly squeezed lemon juice over the salmon balls and you are free to serve the fish balls with a white wine. Remember that this dish should be served warm.

Nutritional Information:
Calories: 322; Total fat: 54 oz; Total carbohydrates: 74 oz; Protein: 38 oz

Salmon Salad with Almonds and Oranges

Prep Time: 10 min. | Cooking Time: 10 min. | Servings: 2

Ingredients:

25 oz smoked salmon, cubed
1 cup of almonds
2 big oranges, peeled and cubed
1 big cucumber, cubed
1 lemon
2 tablespoons lemon zest, minced
Cilantro
Sea salt
freshly ground black pepper

How to Prepare:

1. Preheat the oven to 200°-230°Fahrenheit and roast the almonds in the oven for 10 minutes until lightly browned and crispy and then set aside to cool completely. Then grind the almonds using a food processor or blender.
2. Halve the lemon and then squeeze the fruit.
3. Combine the salmon with all the salad ingredients and pour the lemon juice on top.
4. Portion the salad into two bowls or mugs and you are free to serve the salad. Remember that this dish should be served cool or cold.

Nutritional Information:

Calories: 159; Total fat: 29 oz; Total carbohydrates: 34 oz; Protein: 21 oz

Salmon Balls with Spanish Herbs and Walnuts

Prep Time: 15 min. | Cooking Time: 40 min. | Servings: 4

Ingredients:

30 oz salmon stuffing (grated salmon with spices)
1 teaspoon Pimentón – dried Paprika or Spanish paprika, or pimentón
1 teaspoon Azafrán - Saffron
1 teaspoon Perejil, dried Parsley
1 teaspoon Guindilla - Cayenne Pepper
Laurel (Bay Leaf)
1 cup of walnuts
5 tablespoons Olive oil
5 tablespoons freshly squeezed lemon juice
1 teaspoon powdered red pepper
2 tablespoons powdered garlic
salt and pepper
dill, chopped

How to Prepare:

1. Preheat the oven to 200°-230°Fahrenheit and roast the walnuts in the oven for 10 minutes until lightly browned and crispy and then set aside to cool completely. Then grind the walnuts using a food processor or blender.
2. In a bowl, combine powdered red pepper, powdered garlic, Spanish herbs and some salt. Mix well. Mix in the walnuts.
3. Form the salmon balls out of the ground fish mixture. Spoon the salmon balls into the baking pan.

4. Preheat the oven to 320°-360° Fahrenheit, and bake the salmon balls for around 30-40 minutes until golden brown.
5. Sprinkle the salt and pepper and pour the freshly squeezed lemon juice over the salmon balls and you are free to serve the fish balls with a white wine. Remember that this dish should be served warm.

Nutritional Information:

Calories: 357; Total fat: 51 oz; Total carbohydrates: 67 oz; Protein: 35 oz

Salmon with Noodles, Tomatoes and Romano Cheese

Prep Time: 20 min. | Cooking Time: 45 min. | Servings: 4

Ingredients:

30 oz salmon, diced
15 oz short noodles or pasta (e.g. fusilli, macaroni, penne) or a selection of your choice
5 cherry tomatoes
2 packs (16 oz) Romano cheese, grated
5 garlic cloves
Sea salt
3 tablespoons Olive oil
1 lemon
Black ground pepper
Herbs de Provence

4 teaspoons basil

How to Prepare:

1. Boil the water and cook the noodles for 15 minutes (or follow the cooking time suggested on the packet). Add in 1 tablespoon oil. Add 2 tablespoons olive oil when the noodles are ready.
2. In frying pan, heat the oil and fry the salmon and garlic for 20 minutes, then add in the tomatoes.
3. Add the pasta, stir well. If the sauce and salmon is too thick, you should add some hot water.
4. Halve the lemon and then squeeze it.
5. Sprinkle some lemon juice over the salmon and noodles. Add the Herbs de Provence, sea salt, pepper. Top with the grated Romano cheese and stew for 5 minutes on a low heat with the lid closed to melt the cheese.
6. Serve the noodles and salmon with the all sorts of wine.

Nutritional Information:

Calories: 247; Total fat: 36 oz; Total carbohydrates: 43 oz; Protein: 27 oz

Salmon with Spaghetti and Pears

Prep Time: 20 min. | Cooking Time: 45 min. | Servings: 4

Ingredients:
25 oz salmon, diced
2 medium pears, diced
15 oz spaghetti
Sea salt
3 tablespoons Olive oil
1 lemon
Black ground pepper
1 teaspoon nutmeg

How to Prepare:

1. Boil the water and cook the spaghetti for 15 minutes (or follow the cooking time suggested on the packet). Add 2 tablespoons olive oil when the spaghetti are ready.
2. In frying pan, heat the oil and fry the salmon and garlic for 20 minutes, then add in the pears.
3. Add the spaghetti, stir well. If the salmon mixture is too thick, you should add some hot water.
4. Halve the lemon and then squeeze it.
5. Sprinkle some lemon juice over the salmon and spaghetti. Add in the nutmeg, sea salt and pepper.
6. Serve the spaghetti, pears and salmon with the white wine.

Nutritional Information:
Calories: 244; Total fat: 35 oz; Total carbohydrates: 45 oz; Protein: 32 oz

Beans with Salmon, Pork and Cucumbers

Prep Time: 20 min. | Cooking Time: 50 min. | Servings: 3

Ingredients:

2 cups of dry beans
10 oz pork, sliced
2 carrots, peeled and diced
20 oz salmon, diced
1 small celery, peeled and diced
3 cups of water
1 medium cucumber, peeled and sliced
1 medium onion, peeled and chopped
2 garlic cloves, minced
1 bouillon cube
2 tablespoons sunflower oil
1 tablespoon chili powder
½ a teaspoon of cayenne pepper
1 teaspoon of cumin
1 bunch of parsley
salt, to taste
pepper, to taste

How to Prepare:

1. Soak the beans in the warm water for overnight and then heat the water and boil the beans for around 15 minutes until half-cooked.
2. In a bowl, combine the chili powder, cumin, some salt, and pepper. Season the pork and salmon with the chili powder, cumin, salt, and pepper mix. Marinate the pork and the salmon for at least 3 hours but no longer

than 10 hours unrefrigerated at room temperature or place in the fridge.
3. In a skillet, heat some sunflower oil. Add in the salmon, pork, garlic and onions to fry for 5 minutes until clear and caramelized.
4. Add in all the remaining ingredients, except the cucumbers.
5. Close the lid and cook on a low heat for 25-30 minutes.
6. Portion the salmon, pork, beans and vegetables into three bowls or plates and dollop each bowl with the chopped parsley. Remember that this dish should be served warm. Serve the spicy beans, pork and salmon with the white wine.

Nutritional Information:

Calories: 309; Total fat: 50 oz; Total carbohydrates: 60 oz; Protein: 40 oz

Baked Salmon with Zucchini Spaghetti and Cottage Cheese

Prep Time: 10 min. | Cooking Time: 30 min. | Servings: 3

Ingredients:

20 oz salmon, cubed

2 zucchinis, peeled and spiralized

2 cups of Cottage cheese

2 fresh tomatoes, cubed

5 tablespoons Olive oil

5 tablespoons freshly squeezed lemon juice

1 teaspoon powdered red pepper

2 tablespoons powdered garlic

1 teaspoon nutmeg, ground

salt and pepper

1 apple, cubed

How to Prepare:

1. In a bowl, combine powdered red pepper, powdered garlic, nutmeg, pepper, and some salt. Toss the salmon in the powdered garlic, powdered red pepper, salt, pepper and nutmeg mix. Set the salmon aside for at least 1 hour unrefrigerated at room temperature or place in the fridge for few hours.
2. Toss the spiralized zucchini in the Olive oil and salt. Preheat the oven to 300°-320° Fahrenheit, and then bake the salmon and zucchini for around 30 minutes until golden brown. Ten minutes before the zucchini is ready add the cubed tomatoes and bake them with the zucchini stripes.
3. Sprinkle the salt and pepper and pour the freshly squeezed lemon juice over the salmon and vegetables. Portion the salmon and vegetables into three bowls or plates and dollop each plate with the Cottage cheese. Serve the zucchini spaghetti and salmon with the white or red wine. Remember that this dish should be served warm.

Nutritional Information:
Calories: 242; Total fat: 51 oz; Total carbohydrates: 42 oz; Protein: 24 oz

Salmon Balls with Onions

Prep Time: 15 min. | Cooking Time: 50 min. | Servings: 4

Ingredients:
30 oz salmon stuffing
1 cup of cashews
5 tablespoons Olive oil
4 onions, peeled and chopped
5 tablespoons cream
1 teaspoon powdered red pepper
2 tablespoons powdered garlic
1 teaspoon Herbs de Provence
salt and pepper

How to Prepare:

1. Preheat the oven to 200°-230° Fahrenheit and roast the cashews in the oven for 10 minutes until lightly browned and crispy and then set aside to cool completely. Then grind the cashews using a food processor or blender.
2. In a bowl, combine powdered red pepper, powdered garlic, Herbs de Provence, and some salt. Mix well. Mix in the chopped onions and cashews.
3. Form the salmon balls out of the ground fish mixture. Spoon the salmon balls into the baking pan.
4. Preheat the oven to 320°-360° Fahrenheit, and bake the salmon balls for around 30-40 minutes until golden brown.
5. Sprinkle the salt and pepper and spoon the cream over the salmon balls and you are free to serve the

fish balls with the white wine. Remember that this dish should be served warm.

Nutritional Information:

Calories: 285; Total fat: 49 oz; Total carbohydrates: 62 oz; Protein: 35 oz

Marinated Salmon with Nutmeg

Prep Time: 20 min. | *Servings: 2*

Ingredients:
2 salmon fillets, sliced
10 garlic cloves, minced
2-3 teaspoons Sea salt
2 teaspoons garlic powder
1 teaspoon black pepper
2 lemons
1 teaspoon nutmeg

How to Prepare:
1. In a bowl, combine the spices: nutmeg, sea salt, garlic powder and black pepper. Mix the spices well. Toss the salmon slices with the sea salt, garlic powder, black pepper and minced garlic. Mix the salmon slices well.
2. Place the salmon into the plastic kitchen storage container. Halve the lemons and then squeeze them.
3. Pour the lemon juice over the salmon slices and marinate the salmon for at least 20-24 hours in the fridge with the lid closed.
4. Eat the salmon with the sliced baguette or white bread, butter and chives.

Nutritional Information:
Calories: 194; Total fat: 45 oz; Total carbohydrates: 55 oz; Protein: 31 oz

Salmon with Beets and Walnuts and Garlic

Prep Time: 10 min. | Cooking Time: 30 min. | Servings: 2

Ingredients:

20 oz smoked salmon, cubed
3 medium beets
5 garlic cloves, minced
1 cup of walnuts
4 tablespoons mayonnaise
1 medium lemon
2 teaspoons sesame seeds oil
salt and pepper
fresh parsley, chopped

How to Prepare:

1. Preheat the oven to 250°-270°Fahrenheit and roast the walnuts in the oven for 10 minutes until lightly browned and crispy and then set aside to cool

completely. Then grind the walnuts using a food processor or blender.

2. In a saucepan, heat the water and boil the beets over medium heat for around 30 minutes until soft. Cool the beets by placing them in the cold water for 10 minutes and then peel and spiralize them.
3. In a bowl, combine the beets, garlic cloves, salt, pepper and chopped parsley, and mix well. Add in the mayonnaise and salmon and mix well.
4. Halve the lemon and then squeeze it.
5. Pour the sesame seeds oil over the beets salad and sprinkle the walnuts on top. Place the beets and salmon salad in the fridge for 1 hour. Portion the beets and salmon into two plates or bowls and dollop each plate with the freshly squeezed lemon juice.

Nutritional Information:

Calories: 179; Total fat: 44 oz; Total carbohydrates: 37 oz; Protein: 26 oz

Salmon with Pumpkin and Romano Cheese

Prep Time: 10 min. | Cooking Time: 30 min. | Servings: 3

Ingredients:

20 oz salmon, cubed
2 cups of cubed pumpkin
1 small bowl of Romano cheese, grated (around 8 oz)
2 fresh tomatoes, cubed
5 tablespoons Olive oil
5 tablespoons freshly squeezed lemon juice
1 teaspoon powdered red pepper
2 tablespoons powdered garlic
1 teaspoon nutmeg, ground
salt and pepper

How to Prepare:

1. In a bowl, combine powdered red pepper, powdered garlic, nutmeg, pepper, and some salt. Toss the salmon in the powdered garlic, powdered red pepper, salt, pepper and nutmeg mix. Set the salmon aside for at least 1 hour unrefrigerated at room temperature or place in the fridge for few hours.

2. Toss the pumpkin in the Olive oil and salt. Preheat the oven to 300°-320° Fahrenheit, and then bake the salmon and pumpkin for around 30 minutes until golden brown and caramelized. 10 minutes before the salmon and pumpkin are ready add in the grated Romano cheese and cubed tomatoes and bake them with the salmon.

3. Sprinkle the salt and pepper and pour the freshly squeezed lemon juice over the salmon and

vegetables. Portion the salmon and vegetables into three bowls or plates. Serve the salmon and pumpkin with the white or red wine. Remember that this dish should be served warm.

Nutritional Information:
Calories: 194; Total fat: 54 oz; Total carbohydrates: 45 oz; Protein: 25 oz

Lentils with Salmon and Cucumbers

Prep Time: 20 min. | Cooking Time: 50 min. | Servings: 3

Ingredients:

2 cups of lentils
2 carrots, peeled and diced
20 oz salmon, diced
1 small celery, peeled and diced
3 cups of water
2 cucumbers, peeled and diced
1 medium onion, peeled and chopped
2 garlic cloves, minced
1 beef bouillon cube
2 tablespoons sunflower oil
1 tablespoon chili powder
½ a teaspoon of cayenne pepper
1 teaspoon of cumin
1 bunch of parsley
salt, to taste
pepper, to taste

How to Prepare:

1. Soak the lentils in the warm water for overnight and then heat the water and boil the lentils for around 15 minutes until half-cooked.
2. In a bowl, combine the chili powder, cumin, some salt and pepper. Season the salmon with the chili powder, cumin, salt, and pepper mix. Marinate the salmon for at least 3 hours but no longer than 10 hours unrefrigerated at room temperature or place in the fridge.

3. In a skillet, heat some sunflower oil. Add in the salmon, garlic and onions to fry for 5 minutes until clear and caramelized.
4. Add in all the remaining ingredients except the cucumber.
5. Pour some water and close the lid to cook on a low heat for 25-30 minutes.
6. Portion the salmon, lentils and vegetables into three bowls or plates and dollop each bowl with the chopped parsley and cucumber. Remember that this dish should be served warm. Serve the spicy lentils and salmon with the white wine.

Nutritional Information:

Calories: 342; Total fat: 48 oz; Total carbohydrates: 59 oz; Protein: 34 oz

Chickpeas with Salmon, Bell Peppers and Cress

Prep Time: 20 min. | Cooking Time: 75 min. | Servings: 3

Ingredients:

2 cups of chickpeas
2 carrots, peeled and diced
20 oz salmon, diced
2 medium onions, peeled and chopped
3 bell peppers, chopped
5 cherry tomatoes, chopped
3 cups of water
2 garlic cloves, minced
1 vegetable bouillon cube
2 tablespoons Olive oil
1 teaspoon of oregano
1 bunch of parsley
salt, to taste
pepper, to taste

How to Prepare:

1. Soak the chickpeas in the warm water for overnight and then heat the water and boil the chickpeas for around 25 minutes until half-cooked.
2. In a bowl, combine the oregano, 2/3 parsley, some salt and pepper. Mash the spices well. Season the salmon with the oregano, parsley, salt, and pepper mix. Marinate the salmon for at least 3 hours unrefrigerated at room temperature or place in the fridge overnight.
3. In a skillet, heat some Olive oil. Fry the onions on a low heat for 15 minutes until clear and caramelized. Mix in the chopped cherry tomatoes and stew for 5 minutes with the lid closed.
4. Add in the salmon and garlic to fry for 10 minutes until golden brown.
5. Add in all the remaining ingredients.
6. Pour some water and add the vegetables bouillon cube. Cook on a low heat for 25-30 minutes with the lid closed.
7. Portion the salmon, chickpeas and vegetables into three bowls or mugs and dollop each bowl with the fresh and green cress. Remember that this dish should be served warm. Serve the chickpeas and salmon with the beer.

Nutritional Information:
Calories: 352; Total fat: 54 oz; Total carbohydrates: 60 oz; Protein: 36 oz

Salmon and Veal Cubes with Walnuts in Wine

Prep Time: 20 min. | Cooking Time: 70 min. | Servings: 3

Ingredients:

20 oz salmon, cubed
10 oz veal
1 cup of walnuts
1 cup of young red wine
4 carrots, peeled and chopped
5 tablespoons mayonnaise
3 big onions, chopped
4 tablespoons white flour
8 tablespoons pumpkin seeds oil
1 teaspoon basil, dried
1 teaspoon nutmeg
salt and pepper, taste
1 lemon

How to Cook:

1. Preheat the oven to 250°-270°Fahrenheit and roast the walnuts in the oven for 10 minutes until lightly browned and crispy and then set aside to cool completely. Then grind the walnuts using a food processor or blender.
2. In a bowl, combine the nutmeg, basil, some salt and pepper. Season the cubed salmon and veal with the spices mix, and toss in the mayonnaise. Set the salmon and veal cubes aside to marinate them for at least few hours unrefrigerated at

room temperature or place in the fridge overnight.

3. In a deep skillet or wok, heat the pumpkin seeds oil and stew the veal and salmon chunks on a medium heat for 20 minutes with the lid closed.
4. Then spoon in the walnuts carrots and onions and then mix in the white flour and pour some young red wine. Add in all the remaining ingredients.
5. Stew the salmon, veal and vegetables on a low heat for 30-40 minutes with the lid closed.
6. Meanwhile, halve the lemon and then squeeze the fruit.
7. Portion the salmon, veal and vegetables into three bowls or plates and sprinkle each bowl with the lemon juice. Remember that this dish should be served warm. Serve the cabbage, salmon and veal with the crispy baguette.

Nutritional Information:
Calories: 350; Total fat: 55 oz; Total carbohydrates: 65 oz;

Protein: 45 oz

Pancakes with Kippered Salmon and Chives

Prep Time: 20 min.	Cooking Time: approx. 30 min.
	Servings: 4

Ingredients:
2 salmon fillets, sliced
2-3 teaspoons Sea salt
1 teaspoon black pepper
2 lemons
0.5 teaspoon oregano
2 tablespoons soy sauce
1 bunch of chives, chopped

For Pancakes:
4 eggs
1 cup of plain flour
1 tablespoon sunflower or sesame seeds oil
4 tablespoons sunflower oil for frying
A bit of salt and sugar
1 cup of milk or water
half teaspoon baking soda or baking powder

How to Prepare:
1. In a bowl, combine the spices: sea salt, black pepper and oregano. Mix the spices well. Sprinkle the salmon slices with the sea salt, black pepper and oregano. Sprinkle the salmon slices on all sides.
2. Place the salmon into the plastic kitchen storage container. Halve the lemons and then squeeze them.
3. Pour the lemon juice over the salmon slices and marinate the salmon for at least 20-24 hours in the fridge.

4. Next day, in a bowl, beat the eggs until foamy using an electric hand mixer. Then mix in the flour, milk, salt, sugar and baking soda or baking powder. Whisk all the ingredients well until creamy consistency and homogenous mass. Then set aside for 20 minutes.
5. Set the frying pan over a low heat and heat the sunflower oil for 3-5 minutes.
6. Cook the pancakes for around 2 minutes on each side until crispy and golden brown. Keep your pancakes warm.
7. Wrap the salmon and chives into the pancakes and sprinkle some soy sauce on top.
8. Portion the pancakes, chives and salmon into four bowls or plates. Remember that the pancakes with the kippered salmon should be served warm. Serve the pancakes and salmon with tea or coffee.

Nutritional Information:

Calories: 194; Total fat: 41 oz; Total carbohydrates: 57 oz; Protein: 33 oz

Pancakes with Kippered Salmon and Lettuce

Prep Time: 20 min.	Cooking Time: approx. 30 min.
	Servings: 4

Ingredients:
2 salmon fillets, sliced
15 oz lettuce
2-3 teaspoons Sea salt
1 teaspoon black pepper
2 lemons
0.5 teaspoon oregano
2 tablespoons soy sauce

For Pancakes:
4 eggs
1 cup of plain flour
1 tablespoon sunflower or sesame seeds oil
4 tablespoons sunflower oil for frying
A bit of salt and sugar
1 cup of milk or water

half teaspoon baking soda or baking powder

How to Prepare:

1. In a bowl, combine the spices: sea salt, black pepper and oregano. Mix the spices well. Sprinkle the salmon slices with the sea salt, black pepper and oregano. Sprinkle the salmon slices on all sides.
2. Place the salmon into the plastic kitchen storage container. Halve the lemons and then squeeze them.
3. Pour the lemon juice over the salmon slices and marinate the salmon for at least 20-24 hours in the fridge.
4. Next day, in a bowl, beat the eggs until foamy using an electric hand mixer. Then mix in the flour, milk, salt, sugar and baking soda or baking powder. Whisk all the ingredients well until creamy consistency and homogenous mass. Then set aside for 20 minutes.
5. Set the frying pan over a low heat and heat the sunflower oil for 3-5 minutes.
6. Cook the pancakes for around 2 minutes on each side until crispy and golden brown. Keep your pancakes warm.
7. Wrap the salmon and lettuce leaves into the pancakes and sprinkle some soy sauce on top.
8. Portion the pancakes with the lettuce and salmon into four bowls or plates. Remember that the pancakes with the kippered salmon and lettuce should be served warm. Serve the pancakes and salmon with tea or coffee.

Nutritional Information:

Calories: 202; Total fat: 44 oz; Total carbohydrates: 58 oz; Protein: 35 oz

Pancakes with Smoked Salmon

Prep Time: 20 min.	Cooking Time: approx. 30 min. Servings: 4

Ingredients:
20 oz smoked salmon, cubed
2-3 teaspoons Sea salt
1 teaspoon black pepper
2 lemons
2 tablespoons soy sauce

For Pancakes:
4 eggs
1 cup of plain flour
1 tablespoon sunflower or sesame seeds oil
4 tablespoons sunflower oil for frying
A bit of salt and sugar
1 cup of milk or water
half teaspoon baking soda or baking powder

How to Prepare:
1. Place the salmon into the plastic kitchen storage container or bowl. Halve the lemons and then squeeze them.
2. Pour the lemon juice over the salmon slices and marinate the salmon for at least 20 minutes.
3. Next day, in a bowl, beat the eggs until foamy using an electric hand mixer. Then mix in the flour, milk, salt, sugar and baking soda or baking powder. Whisk all the ingredients well until creamy

consistency and homogenous mass. Then set aside for 20 minutes.

4. Set the frying pan over a low heat and heat the sunflower oil for 3-5 minutes.
5. Cook the pancakes for around 2 minutes on each side until crispy and golden brown. Keep your pancakes warm.
6. Wrap the salmon into the pancakes and sprinkle some soy sauce on top.
7. Portion the pancakes and salmon into four bowls or plates. Remember that the pancakes with the salmon should be served warm. Serve the pancakes and salmon with tea or coffee.

Nutritional Information:
Calories: 195; Total fat: 40 oz; Total carbohydrates: 56 oz; Protein: 32 oz

Pancakes with Salmon and Parsley

Prep Time: 20 min.	Cooking Time: approx. 30 min.
	Servings: 4

Ingredients:
15 oz smoked salmon, cubed
2-3 teaspoons Sea salt
1 teaspoon black pepper
2 lemons
0.5 teaspoon oregano
2 tablespoons soy sauce
1 bunch of parsley, chopped

For Pancakes:
4 eggs
1 cup of plain flour
1 tablespoon sunflower or sesame seeds oil
4 tablespoons sunflower oil for frying
A bit of salt and sugar
1 cup of milk or water
half teaspoon baking soda or baking powder

How to Prepare:
1. In a bowl, combine the spices: sea salt, black pepper and oregano. Mix the spices well. Sprinkle the salmon slices with the sea salt, black pepper and oregano. Sprinkle the salmon slices on all sides.
2. Place the salmon into the plastic kitchen storage container. Halve the lemons and then squeeze them.

3. Pour the lemon juice over the salmon slices and marinate the salmon for at least 20-24 hours in the fridge.
4. Next day, in a bowl, beat the eggs until foamy using an electric hand mixer. Then mix in the flour, milk, salt, sugar and baking soda or baking powder. Whisk all the ingredients well until creamy consistency and homogenous mass. Then set aside for 20 minutes.
5. Set the frying pan over a low heat and heat the sunflower oil for 3-5 minutes.
6. Cook the pancakes for around 2 minutes on each side until crispy and golden brown. Keep your pancakes warm.
7. Wrap the salmon and parsley into the pancakes and sprinkle some soy sauce on top.
8. Portion the pancakes, parsley and salmon into four bowls or plates. Remember that the pancakes with the salmon should be served warm. Serve the pancakes and salmon with tea.

Nutritional Information:

Calories: 192; Total fat: 40 oz; Total carbohydrates: 54 oz; Protein: 31 oz

Salmon with Italian Spaghetti and Grana Padano Cheese

Prep Time: 25 min. | Cooking Time: 85 min. | Servings: 4

Ingredients:

40 oz salmon, diced
spaghetti (around 20 oz)
5 medium tomatoes, diced
2 tablespoons garlic butter
10 oz fresh basil leaves, chopped
7 oz rye bread
1 teaspoon herbs
2 onions, peeled and chopped
1 garlic clove, chopped
4 tablespoons white flour
1 cup of milk or cream
7 tablespoons sunflower oil

8 oz Grana Padano cheese, grated
1 cup of white wine
salt and pepper
Herbs de Provence

How to Cook:

1. Boil the water and cook the spaghetti for 20 minutes. (or follow the cooking time suggested on the packet). Add 2 tablespoons garlic butter when the spaghetti is cooked. Later we will use the water from the boiled spaghetti.
2. Cut the rye bread into the small cubes and toss them with the salt and herbs. Preheat the oven to 250°-270° Fahrenheit and spread the rye bread cubes on a baking sheet. Bake the croutons for about 10-15 minutes until golden brown and crispy.
3. In a skillet, heat the oil and fry the salmon for 15-20 minutes. Then mix in the onions, basil and chopped garlic and fry for 10 minutes.
4. Spoon the flour, pour the water from the boiled spaghetti and white wine and cook for 10 min further.
5. Next pour the milk or cream and stew for 10 min with the lid closed.
6. Spoon the spaghetti into the salmon and sauce and add in Herbs de Provence, some salt and pepper and stir well.
7. Grate the Grana Padano cheese on top and add the rye bread croutons. Serve the salmon and spaghetti with the white wine!

Nutritional Information:

Calories: 327; Total fat: 54 oz; Total carbohydrates: 69 oz; Protein: 35 oz

Salmon Heads and Squash Soup

Prep Time: 20 min. | *Cooking Time: 65 min.* | *Servings: 4*

Ingredients:

4 medium salmon heads
1 medium squash, peeled and diced
4 potatoes, peeled and diced
2 onions, peeled and chopped
5 oz white bread, cubed
4 chopped garlic cloves
10 oz unsalted butter
5 tablespoons white flour
2 carrots, peeled and chopped
2 tablespoons soy sauce
2 tablespoons sunflower oil
salt and pepper
Herbs de Provence

How to Cook:

1. In a pot, boil the salmon heads for around 20 minutes. Add in some salt. Remove the foam from the salmon heads soup.
2. In a skillet or wok, melt the unsalted butter and fry the onions for around 10 minutes until clear and caramelized and then add in the flour to stew for the few minutes on a low heat.
3. In a pot with the salmon heads, combine all the vegetables and the butter-onions mixture. Reduce the heat and continue to boil for around 30 minutes but don't forget to skim the foam from the salmon soup.

4. Meanwhile, preheat the oven to 240°-260° Fahrenheit. Cut the white bread into the small cubes and toss them with the salt, pepper and herbs. Place the bread cubes on a baking sheet. Bake the croutons for about 10-15 minutes until golden brown and crispy.
5. Portion the salmon heads and squash soup into four bowls or mugs and dollop each bowl with the herbs. Serve the soup with the wheat bread! Remember that this dish should be served warm.

Nutritional Information:
Calories: 251; Total fat: 54 oz; Total carbohydrates: 62 oz; Protein: 39 oz

Spicy Salmon Heads Bouillon

Prep Time: 20 min. | *Cooking Time: 65 min.* | *Servings: 4*

Ingredients:

4 medium salmon heads
4 potatoes, peeled and diced
2 onions, peeled and chopped
5 oz white bread or baguette, cubed
4 chopped garlic cloves
10 oz unsalted butter
2 carrots, peeled and chopped
2 tablespoons Olive oil
2 small chili peppers
salt and pepper
Herbs de Provence

How to Cook:

1. In a pot, boil the salmon heads for around 20 minutes. Add in some salt. Remove the foam from the salmon heads bouillon.
2. In a skillet or wok, melt the unsalted butter and fry the onions for around 10 minutes until clear and caramelized.
3. In a pot with the salmon heads, combine all the vegetables and spices. Add in the butter-onions mixture. Reduce the heat and continue to boil for around 30 minutes but don't forget to skim the foam from the salmon bouillon.
4. Meanwhile, preheat the oven to 240°-260° Fahrenheit. Cut the white bread into the small cubes and toss them with the salt, pepper and herbs. Place

the bread cubes on a baking sheet. Bake the croutons for about 10-15 minutes until golden brown and crispy.

5. Portion the salmon heads bouillon into four bowls or mugs and dollop each bowl with the herbs and minced garlic. Remember that this dish should be served warm.

Nutritional Information:

Calories: 254; Total fat: 54 oz; Total carbohydrates: 62 oz; Protein: 37 oz

Grilled Salmon with Stewed Vegetables (Cover Recipe)

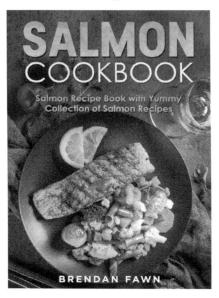

Prep Time: 15 min. | Cooking Time: 45 min. | Servings: 3

Ingredients:

30 oz salmon fillet, cut into pieces
2 glasses of red wine
1 cup of cashews
4 tomatoes cut into rings
1 tablespoon lemon juice
2 tablespoons powdered garlic
5 cloves of garlic, chopped
3 tablespoons Olive oil
3 tablespoons butter, melted
2 tablespoons Herbs de Provence
salt and pepper

Stewed Veggies Ingredients:

  10 oz Brussels sprout
  2 carrots, peeled and cubed
  10 oz broccoli
  10 oz cauliflower
  2 onions, peeled and sliced

How to Cook:

1. Preheat the oven to 250°-270°Fahrenheit and roast the cashews in the oven for 10 minutes until lightly browned and crispy and then set aside to cool completely. Then grind the cashews using a food processor or blender.
2. In a bowl, combine powdered garlic, garlic, some salt, and pepper. Season the salmon with the Herbs de Provence, salt, pepper and garlic mix, and toss in the melted butter. Pour the white wine on top and marinate the salmon for at least 1 hour but no longer than 2 hours unrefrigerated at room temperature or in the fridge.
3. Heat the grill and place the salmon on grill (skin down). Cover the salmon and grill for around 10-20 minutes brushing with the Olive oil or marinade.
4. 10 minutes before the salmon is ready place the few tomatoes on grill.
5. Combine all the stewed vegetables ingredients and boil for 15 minutes.
6. Sprinkle the cashews and lemon juice over the salmon and vegetables and serve with the cold beer.

Nutritional Information:

Calories: 304; Total fat: 48 oz; Total carbohydrates: 57 oz; Protein: 38 oz

Conclusion

Thank you for buying this salmon cookbook. I hope this cookbook was able to help you to prepare fresh and delicious salmon recipes.

If you've enjoyed this salmon cookbook, I'd greatly appreciate if you could leave an honest review on Amazon.

Reviews are very important to us authors, and it only takes a minute for you to post.

Your direct feedback could be used to help other readers to discover the advantages of salmon recipes!

Thank you again and I hope you have enjoyed this cookbook.

Printed in Great Britain
by Amazon